SPORTS MVPs

ALEX MORGAN

BY JAGGER YOUSSEF

Gareth Stevens PUBLISHING

Please visit our website, www.garethstevens.com. For a free color catalog of all our high-quality books, call toll free 1-800-542-2595 or fax 1-877-542-2596.

Library of Congress Cataloging-in-Publication Data

Names: Youssef, Jagger, author.
Title: Alex Morgan / Jagger Youssef.
Description: New York : Gareth Stevens Publishing, [2024] | Series: Sports MVPs | Includes index.
Identifiers: LCCN 2023008951 (print) | LCCN 2023008952 (ebook) | ISBN 9781538285848 (library binding) | ISBN 9781538285831 (paperback) | ISBN 9781538285855 (ebook)
Subjects: LCSH: Morgan, Alex (Alexandra Patricia), 1989—Juvenile literature. | Women soccer players–United States–Biography–Juvenile literature. | FIFA Women's World Cup–History. | Women Olympic athletes–United States–Biography–Juvenile literature.
Classification: LCC GV942.7.M673 Y6 2924 (print) | LCC GV942.7.M673 (ebook) | DDC 796.334092 [B]–dc23/eng/20230306
LC record available at https://lccn.loc.gov/2023008951
LC ebook record available at https://lccn.loc.gov/2023008952

Published in 2024 by
Gareth Stevens Publishing
2544 Clinton St,
Buffalo, NY 14224

Designer: Claire Wrazin
Editor: Therese Shea

Photo credits: Cover, pp. 1, 9 Romain Biard/Shutterstock.com; p. 5 feelphoto/Shutterstock.com; pp. 7, 19 Mikolaj Barbanell/Shutterstock.com; pp. 11, 21 lev radin/Shutterstock.com; pp. 13, 15, 17 Jose Breton- Pics Action/Shutterstock.com.

Printed in the United States of America

CPSIA compliance information: Batch #CS24GS: For further information contact Gareth Stevens, New York, New York at 1-800-542-2595.

CONTENTS

Boldface words appear in the glossary.

Team Player

Alex Morgan is a soccer star. She is a **forward**. She plays on the U.S. women's national team. She also plays in the National Women's Soccer League. Alex is famous for her speed and strength on the field!

VISA

Young Athlete

Alexandra Patricia Morgan was born July 2, 1989, in San Dimas, California. Alex played many sports, including volleyball and track. When she was 14, she joined a soccer team called Cypress Elite. The team won the Under-16 **championship**.

USA

Sharpening Her Skills

Alex also played soccer for Diamond Bar High School. She was named **All-American** by a national group of coaches. She joined teams that prepare players for the Olympics. Playing with different players and coaches helped her get even better.

A Golden Bear

In 2007, Alex began at the University of California, Berkeley. Her soccer team was called the California Golden Bears. Alex led the Golden Bears in goals during each of her four years. The team went to the **NCAA tournament** all four years.

AON
HUBLOT
GENEVE
Baden

Into the Pros

In 2011, Alex was the first pick at the Women's Professional Soccer (WPS) **draft**. She was chosen by the Western New York Flash. She scored a goal in her first game! The Flash won the WPS championship that year.

Alex's **career** has taken her far. She played for the Seattle Sounders, Portland Thorns, and Orlando Pride. In 2017, she played for the French team Olympique Lyonnais. In 2019, she played for the British team Tottenham Hotspur. In 2021, she joined the San Diego Wave.

World Cups

Alex was the youngest player on the 2011 World Cup team. She played in the World Cup again in 2015. In the 2019 World Cup, Alex scored five goals in the team's first game. That tied a record for most goals in a Women's World Cup game! The U.S. team won the World Cup in 2015 and 2019.

USA
15
USA
13

Olympics

Alex played on the U.S. team in the 2012 Olympics. They won a gold medal! Alex played in the 2016 Olympics too. She kicked a goal in the **quarterfinals** to tie the game, but the United States lost. In 2021, Alex and the women's Olympic team placed third.

Alex the Author

Alex is also an author, or writer. She wrote a book series called *The Kicks* for middle school readers. The stories are about playing soccer and working as a team. The stories were made into a TV show. Alex has many talents!

MORE TO KNOW

Alex is 5 feet 7 inches (170 cm) tall.

Alex holds a black belt in **karate**.

Alex's jersey number is 13.

Alex fights for women in sports to be paid the same amount as men.

Alex wrote a book about her life called *Breakaway: Beyond the Goal*.

GLOSSARY

All-American: One of the best in the nation in a certain sport.

career: The job someone chooses to do for a long time.

championship: A contest to decide an overall winner.

draft: The act of picking players for a team.

forward: A player positioned near the opponent's goal, usually a skilled scorer.

karate: A form of fighting developed in Japan in which the feet and hands are used to kick and hit an opponent.

NCAA tournament: A series of games between sports teams in the NCAA (National Collegiate Athletic Association) to decide a champion.

quarterfinals: One of four games to decide the four teams that will continue playing in a tournament.

FOR MORE INFORMATION

BOOKS

Abdo, Kenny. *Alex Morgan.* Minneapolis, MN: Fly!, 2021.

Chandler, Matt. *Alex Morgan: Soccer Champion.* North Mankato, MN: Capstone Press, 2020.

Jökulsson, Illugi. *Stars of Women's Soccer.* New York, NY: Abbeville Press, 2021.

WEBSITES

Alex Morgan
www.biography.com/athletes/alex-morgan
Learn about some notable goals that Alex has scored.

Alex Morgan
www.ussoccer.com/players/m/alex-morgan
Read more about Alex on this USA Soccer website.

INDEX